Building Fluency With Mini-Plays

As you may well know, fluency is an important aspect of reading. When a student can read text quickly and accurately with meaning and expression, then she can be said to read fluently. But fluent reading is not just about speed; it's also about understanding and interpreting the text. It's about comprehension. When a reader is struggling to sound out words and reads haltingly, he cannot pay attention to the meaning of the text and so cannot comprehend what the text is about. A fluent reader, on the other hand, can focus on the meaning because she is not bogged down by the features of print.

So how can students build fluency? Research shows that repeated reading helps improve word recognition, speed, and phrasal reading—all keys to fluent reading. As with any skill, repeated practice leads to proficiency. So, for students to develop fluency, they need to read a lot!

That's where these read-aloud mini-plays come in. Students inherently want to perform well, so they're motivated to practice reading their parts over and over again until they can read their lines fluently. And, in order to present their characters convincingly to the audience, they need to comprehend their parts as well. To sum up, these mini-plays give students an authentic reason for repeated reading and thereby help them develop fluency and comprehension.

How to Use the Mini-Plays

Divide the class into groups according to the number of characters in the mini-play. You may decide to have different groups of students working on different plays, or have all the groups work on the same play. Make sure you have an equal number of at- or above-level readers and below-level readers in the group. In each group, assign each student a role based on his or her reading level. (Refer to the key on page 64 to help you match characters to students' reading levels.) Then photocopy the mini-play(s) and distribute copies to students.

Try the following steps to make the best use of the read-aloud mini-plays:

1) Model fluency. When introducing a mini-play to students, read aloud the whole play first, making sure to pay close attention to phrasing, pacing, and expression. Students need to hear a model of fluent reading to develop their own fluency skills.

2) Let students practice reading independently. Encourage students to read the script independently so they can focus on the text and identify new vocabulary words and practice decoding unfamiliar words. Help individual students as needed.

3) Give students practice reading in groups. Invite students to practice reading aloud in their groups. When students listen to one another read and get feedback from both their peers and you, their accuracy and fluency improves. As they begin to read automatically, they can start thinking about how to interpret their parts for the audience. Encourage students to think about how to use their voice and actions to make their characters come to life.

4) Have students perform to an audience. This is the moment everybody's been waiting for! Invite each group to stand in front of the class and read aloud its mini-play. Then sit back and enjoy your students' performance.

After all the groups have performed, consider throwing a "cast party" to celebrate your confident and fluent readers!

SCHOLASTIC

READ-ALOUD MINI-PLAYS
with LEVELED PARTS

20 Reproducible High-Interest Plays
That Help Kids at Different Reading Levels Build Fluency

Justin McCory Martin

NEW YORK • TORONTO • LONDON • AUCKLAND • SYDNEY
MEXICO CITY • NEW DELHI • HONG KONG • BUENOS AIRES

Teaching *Resources*

DEDICATION

To Brett, Colleen & Cy,
my Left Coast right-brained relatives

Editor: Maria L. Chang
Cover design by Jason Robinson
Interior design by Grafica, Inc.
Illustrations by Kelly Kennedy

ISBN-13: 978-0-439-87028-3
ISBN-10: 0-439-87028-3
Copyright © 2007 by Justin McCory Martin
All rights reserved.
Printed in the USA.

2 3 4 5 6 7 8 9 10   40   15 14 13 12 11 10 09 08 07

Contents

Introduction

Welcome to *Read-Aloud Mini-Plays With Leveled Parts*. The aim of this book is to get kids jazzed about reading aloud so they can build fluency. Inside, you'll find 20 mini-plays with dialogue for different characters written at two levels of reading difficulty. Chances are, the students in your class vary in their reading proficiency, yet all your different-level readers will be able to participate in these plays together. Even your most reluctant readers are likely to be motivated to "perform" in these highly engaging mini-plays.

This book is divided into four sections: School Situations, Mysteries, Tall Tales, and Just For Laughs. These categories are specifically chosen to appeal to your students. For example, students are likely to relate to the School Situations section, which features characters who might seem familiar. In "The Cool Table," for instance, Sara abandons her best friend Sue to try to break in with the popular crowd. But Sara is in for a surprise. Meanwhile, the Just For Laughs section includes the mini-play "The Fearsome Four vs. the Giant Paperboy From Outer Space." Obviously, this is very different dramatic fare than the plays in the Mysteries or Tall Tales section.

Each mini-play features about six to eight characters. In each play, the dialogue for half of the characters rates between 1.0 and 2.9 on the Spache Readability Index. (Spache is a respected and widely used method for measuring the relative difficulty of passages of text.) Dialogue for the other characters rates between 3.0 and 4.9 on the Spache index. But you won't necessarily be able to tell which characters are at what level. More important, neither will your students. This is by design. In a given play, a Level 1 character (1.0 to 2.9 on the Spache index) might get a long stretch of dialogue, while a Level 2 character (3.0 to 4.9) might get a shorter piece but with more challenging vocabulary words. A key at the back of the book will help you discretely match characters to students' reading levels. This way, all students will be able to read their parts comfortably and, in the process, build their confidence and fluency. Everyone will benefit from this shared experience.

The New Kid

Characters
- Narrator 1
- Narrator 2
- Fran
- Hannah
- Danielle
- Chris

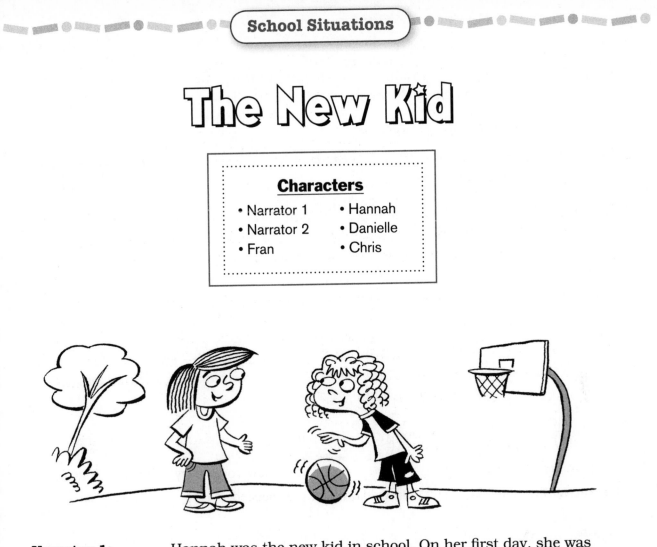

Narrator 1: Hannah was the new kid in school. On her first day, she was very nervous. All the other kids knew each other really well. They all seemed to fit right in.

Narrator 2: Hannah wondered if she would ever make friends. The first person Hannah met was Fran. Fran was known as a big talker.

Fran: Where did you move here from? Do you live close to the school? How do you like it so far? Who is your closest, most super-special new friend? Do you have any really juicy gossip? Don't hold anything back. Tell me absolutely everything.

Hannah: I moved here from across town. This seems like a really great school so far.

Narrator 1: That was all Hannah could think of to say. She wasn't sure exactly how to talk to Fran yet. Meanwhile, Fran caught up with her friends Danielle and Chris. Fran shared what she had learned about the new kid.

Fran:	That Hannah sure doesn't have much to say. Maybe she's shy. Maybe she's stuck on herself. She is as quiet as a teeny little mouse.
Narrator 2:	The next person Hannah met was Danielle. Danielle was great at sports.
Danielle:	We are playing basketball at recess. We need another person so that the teams will be even. You look like you would be good at basketball. Do you want to play?
Hannah:	I'm not sure. I have never played before.
Narrator 1:	Hannah wished she hadn't said that. She realized she should have simply said yes. Meanwhile, Danielle caught up with her friends Fran and Chris. Danielle shared what she had learned about the new kid.
Danielle:	I will tell you one thing. This new girl has never even played basketball. She must be bad at sports.
Narrator 2:	The next person Hannah met was Chris. He was the class clown.
Chris:	Look at me, look at me. I can cross my eyes and touch my tongue to my nose at the same time. Now I'm doing it standing on one leg. Do you want me to do it while floating in the air?
Hannah:	I guess so. Can you really do that?
Narrator 1:	Hannah was embarrassed. She certainly knew Chris couldn't float in the air with his eyes crossed and his tongue touching his nose. But she had just met him. Meanwhile, Chris caught up with his friends Fran and Danielle. Chris shared what he had learned about the new kid.
Chris:	I made this really wacky face. Then I said I was going to float in the air. I think she believed me. That new girl has no sense of humor.
Narrator 2:	All the kids decided to play soccer at recess instead of basketball. Hannah was glad. She was good at soccer. She even hit the ball with her head. She scored a goal that way.

Hannah: That was fun. I think I really used my head. We are winning by just one goal now. Let's keep the other team from scoring.

Narrator 1: The kids saw a different side of Hannah now.

Fran: She doesn't seem so terribly shy.

Danielle: I think she is pretty good at sports.

Chris: I cracked up when she said, "I really used my head." I think she's pretty funny, too. Hey, Hannah, do you want to have lunch with us tomorrow?

Hannah: I am very busy tomorrow. I am climbing the world's tallest mountain. At the top I am giving a speech to a thousand people. Just kidding! I would love to have lunch with you, Danielle, and Fran.

Narrator 2: Hannah was already starting to fit in. By the end of her first day of school she had three new friends.

The Cool Table

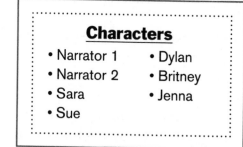

> ## Characters
> - Narrator 1
> - Narrator 2
> - Sara
> - Sue
> - Dylan
> - Britney
> - Jenna

Narrator 1: Sara did everything with Sue. She always sat beside Sue on the bus to school. They laughed together. They shared secrets together.

Narrator 2: Sara and Sue were best friends. They even finished each other's sentences.

Sara: Could you believe what happened in class this morning? Theo brought his pet snake to school. It escaped from his backpack and it was so...

Sue: Disgusting. That snake was crawling all over the floor and it even slithered right over one of my feet. Did you see Jimmy jump on top of his desk? His hair was standing on end, I swear, and he looked like he was about to start screaming.

Narrator 1: Sara had so much fun with Sue. But there was one small problem. Sara wanted to be one of the cool kids. Those kids all ate lunch together. They sat at the cool table.

Narrator 2:	Sara knew that Sue would not be interested. Sue did not seem to even notice the cool table. Sara would just have to leave her friend behind. She decided to join those kids on her own.
Sara:	Is it okay if I eat lunch at your table? Can I sit down in that empty chair?
Dylan:	Have a seat.
Narrator 1:	Sara was really at the cool table! She could not believe her good luck. The other kids were all talking. Sara wanted to join in.
Britney:	Who saw *Robin's World* on TV last night? My favorite part was when Robin dumped spaghetti on her little brother's head. Then her mother said, "You are grounded, young lady." So Robin said, "How long this time?" Her mother said, "Until your hair is blue and you walk with a cane." That was hilarious!
Narrator 2:	Sara did not have anything to say. Sara did not watch *Robin's World*. She and Sue always watched *Loopy Lane*. Then the kids at the table started talking about sports.
Dylan:	That was an awesome basketball game in gym today. I made so many shots. I think you had almost as many points, Britney. I kept blocking your shots, Jenna. I am the champ!
Narrator 1:	Sara wanted to join in, but she did not like basketball. She and Sue always played soccer. Sara had nothing to say. Then Jenna started talking about nail polish.
Jenna:	I did my thumbs in pink. See? Then I did three of my fingers in the brightest red that I could find. Doesn't this just scream *RED*? Then I did my pinkies in yellow. Can you believe it? I didn't even know yellow nail polish existed. This color is called Summer Sun.
Narrator 2:	Sara wanted to join in. She and Sue did not even wear nail polish. They liked to braid each other's hair. Once again, Sara had nothing to say.

Narrator 1:	Sara decided she would go back to eating lunch with Sue. There was nothing wrong with the kids at the cool table. They were not mean. They were just different from her. They were not really her friends.
Sara:	Hi Sue. You get pudding and I'll get tater tots. We'll each eat half and then we'll trade like we always do. I really want to apologize because…
Sue:	…you thought you'd be happier at the cool table, but you weren't?
Sara:	That's right. Now I see that…
Sue:	…you should have stayed with…
Sara:	…my real friend! Right again, Sue. Thanks for being…
Sue:	…so forgiving. Let's go grab a table. There's a whole bunch of stuff that I can't wait to tell you.
Narrator 2:	Sara had learned her lesson. She and Sue were so happy to be back together. They were even finishing each other's sentences again.

A Rumor Going Around

Characters

- Narrator 1
- Narrator 2
- Davey
- Wanda
- Janie, Wanda's best friend
- Daniel, Davey's best friend

Narrator 1: Davey wanted to figure out a way to impress his classmates. He had an idea. Rumors traveled through his school really fast and they always got everybody talking. He decided to start a rumor about himself.

Narrator 2: Wanda was the best at starting rumors. Davey decided to tell her first.

Davey: I was playing basketball yesterday. I was on fire. I kept making shots. The kids on my team kept passing the ball to me. I was scoring from close to the basket. I was scoring from far away. I was making every single shot. The other kids said they had never seen anything like it. They said I was the best kid basketball player they had ever seen.

Narrator 2: Wanda listened to Davey's story. She could not wait to tell Janie, her best friend. But she changed the story around just a little bit.

Wanda:	You have to hear this, Janie! Yesterday at recess, Davey was playing soccer. His team was losing 8 to nothing. All of a sudden, Davey went on a hot streak. He kicked nine goals right in a row. He kicked the winning goal from all the way across the field. Mr. Sabatino was watching. He said that Davey is better at soccer than a lot of players that are twice his age.
Narrator 2:	Janie listened to the story. She could not wait to tell her friend, Daniel. But she changed the story just slightly.
Janie:	Davey was playing kickball. He kicked the ball really far. It went over the school roof. Mr. Sabatino was watching. He said that no one has ever kicked a ball over the roof in the whole history of the school.
Narrator 2:	Daniel listened to the story. He could not wait to discuss it with his best friend, Davey.
Daniel:	Hey, Davey. I heard you did a monster kick, sent the ball flying completely over the school's roof.
Davey:	It was no big deal. I just gave the ball a good kick.
Narrator 1:	Davey could hardly believe how well it had worked. He had started a rumor about himself and it had turned out way better than he had planned. Now everyone thought he could kick a ball super far. Right then and there, he decided to make up another story and get the rumor mill rolling with Wanda.
Davey:	I was at the mall. I was eating a hamburger. There was a woman sitting at the next table. She told me that she made television ads. She said that I looked like I was enjoying my hamburger. She said that I would be perfect for a hamburger ad. Then a man with a camera came over. He filmed me eating my hamburger. I am going to be the star of a television ad.
Narrator 2:	Wanda listened to Davey's story. She could not wait to tell Janie. But first she changed the story around just the tiniest amount.
Wanda:	You won't believe this, Janie! This is incredible! Davey is going to be the star of his own television show. It's called *Mall Burger*, and it's about a kid who is a space alien. He comes to Earth and opens his own hamburger shop at the mall.

Narrator 2: Janie listened to Wanda's story. She could not wait to tell Daniel. But she changed the story around just a tad.

Janie: Davey is going to be a rock star! His band is called Davey and the Aliens. They are going to play at the mall on Saturday. People who go get free hamburgers.

Narrator 2: Daniel was very surprised to hear this new story about his best friend. Something was not right about the story. A lot was not right about it. Daniel decided to talk with Davey to get to the bottom of things.

Daniel: So I heard that you are a big rock star, now. All the kids are saying that you are going to be playing a concert at the mall on Saturday. There will be free hamburgers for everyone who shows up. Would you like me to play drums? Or maybe I can help with the stage—anything to be part of your big event.

Davey: I think I have some explaining to do.

Narrator 1: What a huge mess! The worst part was that Davey had done it himself. Now all the kids at his school believed he was playing a rock concert at the mall. It was happening on Saturday. Everyone was even expecting free hamburgers! Davey gathered Wanda, Janie, and Daniel.

Davey: Here is a rumor that I want you all to spread. Davey told some stories about himself that were not true. He is not a rock star, and there are no free hamburgers. He apologizes to all his friends. He is now going to tell only the truth. Davey also thinks people should stop spreading rumors.

Narrator 2: The rumor spread very quickly to everyone in school. It was the last rumor those students ever spread!

Extreme Eddy

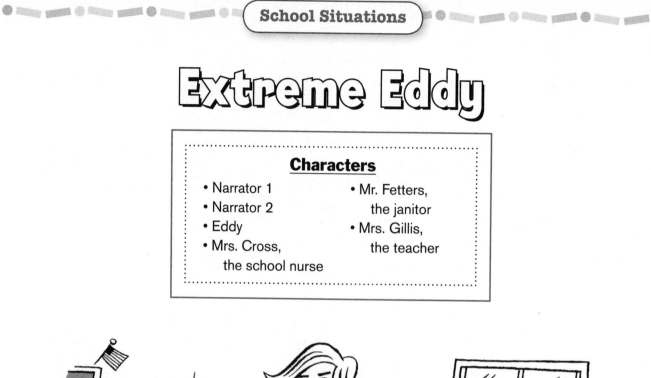

Characters

- Narrator 1
- Narrator 2
- Eddy
- Mrs. Cross, the school nurse
- Mr. Fetters, the janitor
- Mrs. Gillis, the teacher

Narrator 1: Eddy was not mean or a bully. But he still had a habit that got on all the other kids' nerves. Whenever something little happened, Eddy always acted like it was a huge deal. Eddy always took everything to the extreme.

Narrator 2: Eddy was playing a game at recess. He was running after another boy. He fell down and hurt his leg.

Eddy: Oh help! I'm very badly injured. I can't even walk. I think my leg must be broken. I'm losing blood quickly. This is an emergency! Somebody call an ambulance!

Narrator 1: The school nurse came quickly. She only had to glance at Eddy's leg to know that it was just a little scrape.

Mrs. Cross: This is just a small cut, Eddy. There is not much blood at all. Here, let me clean you up and put a bandage on your leg.

Narrator 2: Later that day, Eddy was at lunch. He dropped his tray and spilled all of his food. It went all over the floor.

Eddy: The lunchroom is flooded with chocolate milk! I can see pieces of macaroni bobbing in the milk. What a huge mess! It looks like a tornado hit. It looks like a tornado and a hurricane struck at the same time!

Narrator 1: Eddy caused such a commotion that the school janitor came running. He expected to see a disaster. But all he saw was a small spill.

Mr. Fetters: This is just a spilled lunch tray, Eddy. I thought someone had left the milk machine running. Go and get a new lunch. I'll have this cleaned up in a minute.

Narrator 2: That afternoon, Eddy was walking down a hallway in school. He was carrying his homework. He was by himself. A dog came speeding down the hall. It grabbed his homework and ran off.

Eddy: I can't believe it! A huge dog just came racing down the hall. It snatched my homework in its jaws and ran off. Call the dog pound! There's a wild homework-stealing dog on the loose in our school.

Mrs. Gillis: This is an incredible story, Eddy. You must have worked very hard to dream it up. It would have been easier just to do your homework assignment. You have a very rich imagination, Eddy. Next time, I hope you will put it to good use by doing your homework.

Narrator 1: Eddy realized that Mrs. Gillis did not believe him. A dog really had snatched his homework. He was telling the truth. But Eddy was always too extreme, so people had lost their trust in him.

Narrator 2: Eddy learned his lesson. When something was only a small deal, he did not make it into a big deal. After a while, people started to trust him again. If something big ever happened again, he knew they would believe him now. And Eddy always carried some biscuits in his pocket, just in case he ever saw that dog again.

Borrowing Bob

Characters	
• Narrator	• Jess
• Bob	• Phil
• Jose	• Isabella

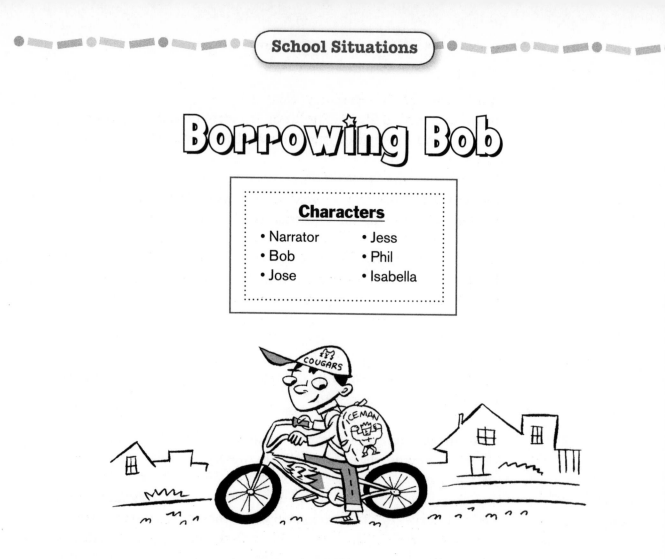

Narrator: Bob enjoyed borrowing stuff from other kids. He borrowed toys, clothes, balls, books, and handheld video-game players. He liked borrowing so much that the kids in school began calling him "Borrowing Bob." Bob loved to borrow just about everything. The problem was that he never gave anything back.

Bob: That is a really awesome bike, Jose! Red is my very favorite color in the whole wide world. It even has flames painted on. Can I borrow your bike?

Jose: You can borrow it for a few minutes. You can take it for a ride around the block. But it is a brand new bike. I got it for my birthday. I have hardly had a chance to ride it yet.

Narrator: So Bob pedaled away on Jose's new red bike with the painted-on flames. He rode around until he ran into Jess.

Bob: That is the best baseball cap, Jess. Blue is my favorite color in the whole wide world. The Cougars are a great team. I'm a big fan and I bet they're going to win the championship. Can I borrow your cap?

Jess: You can borrow it for a while. I'm playing softball later. I need my cap for the game. Make sure to bring it back soon.

Narrator: So Bob pedaled away on Jose's new red bike with the painted-on flames wearing Jess's blue baseball cap. He rode around until he ran into Phil.

Bob: That is the coolest backpack, Phil. It has silver stripes. Silver is my favorite color in the whole wide world. That picture of Ice Man is super cool, too. He's the best superhero. Can I borrow your backpack?

Phil: You can borrow it. It's empty right now. I need it back right away. I'm going to use it later to carry my books.

Narrator: So Bob pedaled away on Jose's new red bike with the painted-on flames wearing Jess's blue baseball cap and Phil's silver-striped backpack. He rode for a long time. The three people Bob had borrowed grew tired of waiting. When he pedaled past them, they got angry. They wanted their stuff back.

Jose: Please give me back my new bike. I want to ride it now.

Bob: Right away, Jose.

Jess: I need you to give me back my cap. My softball game is about to begin.

Bob: In a jiffy, Jess.

Phil: Could you please return my backpack? I need it to carry my books.

Bob: In a flash, Phil.

Narrator: Bob just kept pedaling away on Jose's new red bike with the painted-on flames wearing Jess's blue baseball cap and Phil's silver-striped backpack. He kept riding until he ran into Isabella.

Bob: That's the best watch, Isabella. I saw one exactly like it at the mall. It even has a stopwatch feature. Stopwatches are my favorite kind in the whole wide world. Can I borrow it?

Isabella: You can try out my watch, but only if you do a few things. First, lend me your Game Pal. Then set my stopwatch for one hour. Go give the stuff you borrowed back to Jose, Jess, and Phil. They're really upset. Bring my watch back in an hour. That's when I'll give you back your Game Pal.

Narrator: Bob got the message. He did what Isabella asked and everybody was happy again. After that, he continued to be Borrowing Bob. But he always brought people's stuff back quickly. He also became Lending Bob.

Bob: Hey, can I borrow your green jacket? I'll let you wear my green shoelaces. Green is my favorite color in the whole wide world.

Who Took the Cake?

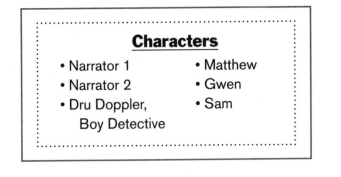

Characters	
• Narrator 1	• Matthew
• Narrator 2	• Gwen
• Dru Doppler, Boy Detective	• Sam

Narrator 1: There was a problem at Stanhope Elementary. A cake had been baked for a class celebration. But someone had eaten that cake. This was a job for Stanhope's most famous student.

Narrator 2: This was a job for Dru Doppler, Boy Detective. Dru called three students into an empty room at the school. Each of them was a suspect. Dru questioned them all.

Dru Doppler: Let's start with you, Matthew. Or should I say, Messy Matthew. I see that you have a very large red food stain on your T-shirt. The missing cake just happens to have cherry icing. I will be quite curious to hear what you have to say.

Matthew: I did not take the cake. This is strawberry ice cream. I got it all over myself.

Narrator 1: Dru paces back and forth across the room. He strokes his chin and appears to be thinking very hard. Then he reaches into his pocket and takes out a piece of candy.

Dru Doppler:	That is a convincing explanation. Hmm... By the way, can I offer you a piece of chocolate?
Matthew:	No, thank you. I am allergic to chocolate.
Dru Doppler:	Now let us move on to you, Gwen. I hear from the school nurse that you have a stomachache. That sounds like the kind of trouble that might strike someone who ate a whole cake with cherry icing. I will be most interested to hear your side of the story.
Gwen:	I do not feel well. My stomach hurts. I have felt sick ever since lunch. But all I ate was pizza.
Narrator 2:	Dru walks across the room again. He still looks like he is thinking hard. He reaches into his pocket. He pulls out a piece of candy.
Dru Doppler:	Hmm... Very interesting. By the way, can I offer you a piece of chocolate?
Gwen:	No, thank you. I think it would make me sick right now. And I don't really like chocolate.
Dru Doppler:	It is time for suspect number three. Sam, I will be very curious to hear your explanation. A cake with cherry icing is missing.
Sam:	Of course it wasn't me! I hate cherry. Ask anyone. I never eat anything that's cherry flavored. I don't even like real cherries. I swear I did not eat that chocolate cake with cherry icing!
Narrator 1:	Dru pauses for a very long time. Now he seems to be concentrating hard. He digs into his pocket. He pulls out a piece of candy and begins slowly unwrapping it.
Dru Doppler:	You make a very convincing argument, Sam.
Sam:	Hey, aren't you going to give me candy? You offered chocolate to the other two.

Dru Doppler: Oh, I very nearly forgot. How rude of me. Would you like a piece of chocolate?

Sam: Absolutely. Boy, that looks delicious!

Dru Doppler: Aha! Now, I know who ate the cake. It was you, Sam. I am 100 percent certain of it.

Sam: Uh... uh... You've got me. I confess. But how did you figure it out?

Dru Doppler: It was simple. I kept saying that the missing cake had cherry icing. But I never said the cake was actually chocolate. Sam, you convinced me that you hate cherry. But you certainly love chocolate. You love it so much that you scraped the cherry icing off the cake and left it on the plate while you gobbled down all the chocolate cake!

Narrator 2: Sam was guilty. As punishment, Sam baked a new cake. This time he ate only one piece.

The Giant of Gumville

> ## Characters
> • Narrator
> • Shirley Holmes,
>   Girl Detective
> • Marc
> • Stu
> • Amber Watson,
>   the deputy
> • Marisa
> • George
> • Emily

Narrator: Marc and Stu were riding their dirt bikes. All of a sudden, they saw a giant. He was huge, easily eight feet tall.

They rode their bikes home, pedaling as fast as possible. They called Shirley Holmes, the famous girl detective. She was the only person in Gumville that could handle a case like this. Shirley came right over with her trusty deputy, Amber Watson.

Shirley Holmes: Tell us exactly what happened. Take your time and try to remember all the important details.

Marc: We were riding our dirt bikes. We saw a giant. He was way taller than a man. He was taking little steps. I think he was coming after us.

Stu: We had to get away! We rode home really fast!

Shirley Holmes: That is a truly bizarre story. I cannot help noticing that you said the giant was taking small steps.

Amber Watson: Why is that important?

Shirley Holmes: I believe it is our first clue.

Narrator: Marisa was shooting baskets in her driveway. Suddenly, the giant came up and snatched the ball. He walked right up and dropped the ball through the hoop. Marisa took out her cell phone and called Girl Detective Shirley Holmes. Shirley came over immediately with her trusty deputy, Amber Watson.

Shirley Holmes: Tell us exactly what happened. Take plenty of time and don't leave anything out.

Marisa: I was playing basketball. This giant showed up and stole the ball. He was wearing a long coat, the kind you wear in winter. The giant dunked the basketball. He was so tall that he did not even have to jump.

Shirley Holmes: That is another truly bizarre story. I cannot help noticing that you said the giant was wearing a long coat.

Amber Watson: Why is that important?

Shirley Holmes: The weather is warm now, so it is strange that the giant is wearing a winter coat. Amber, I believe that is our second clue.

Narrator: George and his sister, Emily, were watching TV. Suddenly, they heard a tapping on the window. That was very strange, because they were on the second floor of their house. They could see a finger tapping and tapping. George tried to be brave. He got to the window just in time to see a giant walking away. Meanwhile, Emily dialed up Girl Detective Shirley Holmes. Shirley arrived immediately, with her trusty deputy, Amber Watson.

Shirley Holmes: Describe the events just as they happened. Think hard and remember that no detail is too small.

George: We heard a finger tapping on the window. I went over to take a look. It was a giant and he was wearing a ski mask. When he saw me, he walked away fast.

Emily: I cannot believe that a big clumsy giant interrupted the very best part of *America's Next Superduperstar*.

Shirley Holmes: That is yet another truly bizarre story. I cannot help noticing that you said the giant was wearing a ski mask.

Amber Watson: What could that mean?

Shirley Holmes: This giant does not want his identity known. That's clue number three. I have a pretty good idea about who we are looking for.

Narrator: Now Detective Shirley Holmes had a plan. She memorized a really funny joke. She practiced it on Amber until she could tell it really well. Then the two of them went to the park. Before very long, they saw the giant walking towards them. Shirley stepped out into the path of the lumbering giant. She told the joke in a loud, clear voice.

Shirley Holmes: Who did the monster bring to the dance?
His ghoul-friend!

Narrator: The giant laughed. In fact, there were two different laughing voices coming from the giant. The two voices kept on giggling. After a while, the giant unbuttoned the winter coat. Inside, were the Timmons twins. One boy was riding on the other boy's shoulders.

Amber Watson: You are amazing, Shirley. How did you figure it out?

Shirley Holmes: Simple, Amber. What kind of giant takes small steps, wears a winter coat in summer, and needs a mask? Case solved. I don't think those Timmons twins will be playing pranks anytime soon.

The DeCrunchy Code

Characters

- Narrator
- Zach
- Rachel
- Voice #1
- Voice #2
- Voice #3

Narrator: The DeCrunchy Code was the biggest mystery in the tiny town of Glendale. First you had to answer three riddles. Then you got a giant candy bar.

Many kids in Glendale had tried to crack the DeCrunchy Code. Nobody had ever succeeded. But Zach thought he could do it. To help him, he brought along his friend, Rachel. He wanted that candy bar.

Zach: I heard that we can get the first clue at the restaurant. What do you think we should do? Should we just go in and ask for some food?

Rachel: Maybe we should ride our bikes into the drive-through. Call it a hunch. But that just seems like a good place to find a clue.

Narrator: Zach and Rachel rode their bikes into the drive-through lane. They pulled up in front of the big menu. They waited until a voice came over the speaker.

Voice #1:	Welcome to DeCrunchy's. Can I help you? Or should I say, can I help you find a candy bar? Listen carefully. Here is your first riddle: *I have teeth, but I cannot eat.*
Zach:	I know. I think it is a person who is not hungry.
Rachel:	That doesn't make a lick of sense, Zach.
Zach:	Sure it does. People have teeth. But if they are not hungry, they cannot eat.
Rachel:	I bet it's a comb. Those little things on a comb are called teeth, and combs definitely can't eat.
Voice #1:	You are right. You got the first riddle. To hear the second riddle, turn your radio to station 88.
Narrator:	Zach and Rachel raced their bikes back to his house. They found a radio and tuned in to station 88. The voice on the radio was different from the one at the restaurant. After a few minutes, the voice began speaking directly to Zach and Rachel.
Voice #2:	Thanks for tuning in to the DeCrunchy Show. Today I have a riddle for our two new listeners: *You are running a race. You pass the person in second place. Now what place are you in?*
Zach:	You would be in first place. That is too easy!
Rachel:	You're right about one thing, Zach. It sounds easy. I'm guessing that it's a trick question. Let's think harder.
Zach:	You are thinking too hard, Rachel. If you pass the person in second place, then you are in first place.
Rachel:	No. If you pass someone who's in second place, it means you were in third place. You've really just switched places. So the correct answer is second place.
Voice #2:	You are right. You have solved the second riddle. To hear the third riddle, go to the park. Wait until no one is close to the big rock. Then walk over to it.

Narrator:	Zach and Rachel ran over to the park. They followed the instructions they had received. When nobody was near the big rock, they walked over. They couldn't believe their ears. A spooky voice seemed to be coming out of the rock.
Voice #3:	I'll bet you have never met a talking rock. I am hard. My riddles are even harder. Good luck figuring out this one: *How do you spell the word* candy *using only two letters?*
Zach:	That is impossible. I was so close. I almost had that candy bar. I can't believe it!
Rachel:	You aren't just going to give up, Zach. Come on. Let's really concentrate.
Zach:	You can't get candy from just two letters. It just can't be done.
Rachel:	Hold on. I think I've figured it out. C and Y! Do you get it? "C and Y" are just two letters. Put it all together and it spells *candy*!
Voice #3:	Congratulations! You have cracked the DeCrunchy Code. There is a tree nearby with a hollow spot. Go and look inside.
Narrator:	Zach sped over to the tree. Sure enough, there was a hollow spot. He reached in his arm and fished around. He found the giant candy bar and pulled it out. He began to unwrap it. It looked really tasty.
Rachel:	Not so fast, buster! I have one last riddle for you: *What is half of a candy bar?*
Zach:	I don't know.
Rachel:	Half of a candy bar is what you owe me. I gave you a ton of help. Wow, that really does look delicious. Now break it in half!

Annelise, the Animal Detective

Characters

- Narrator 1
- Narrator 2
- Jules, the butler
- Mr. Moneypenny
- Annelise, the Animal Detective
- Polly, the parrot

Narrator 1:	Somebody had broken into Mr. Moneypenny's mansion. They had opened a safe and made away with some jewels. First, Mr. Moneypenny called the police. But they could not solve the crime.
Narrator 2:	So he called Annelise, the Animal Detective. She arrived at his home and knocked on the huge door. Inside, a dog started barking. Annelise waited a few minutes until somebody answered.
Jules:	Good evening. I'm sorry it took me so long. I normally answer the door pronto! Whom do I have the pleasure of greeting?
Annelise:	My name is Annelise. I am here to meet with Mr. Moneypenny.
Jules:	Why don't you have a seat in the drawing room. I will let Mr. Moneypenny know that you are here. I expect that he will be down, pronto.

Narrator 1: Jules the Butler walked up a large staircase. Annelise was left in the drawing room. The dog was also there. Annelise was extremely good with animals. She petted and played with the dog until Mr. Moneypenny came downstairs.

Mr. Moneypenny: Hello. You must be Annelise, the world-famous animal detective. I'm most pleased to make your acquaintance.

Annelise: Let's get started. I have a question for you about your dog. Does he bark a lot? Does he only bark when strangers are coming into your home?

Mr. Moneypenny: This is Crawford. I can assure you, he only barks around strangers.

Annelise: I see. Did he bark on the night of the robbery?

Mr. Moneypenny: No, I am most certain that he didn't. He was sleeping soundly at the foot of my bed.

Annelise: It sounds like the robber was not a stranger. Maybe it was someone that Crawford knows. Do you have any other pets?

Mr. Moneypenny: I have a talkative parrot named Polly.

Annelise: I would like to speak with Polly.

Narrator 2: Mr. Moneypenny led Annelise to another room. In that room, there was a cage covered in a blanket. Mr. Moneypenny lifted the blanket and Polly began to talk. Annelise reached into her purse and pulled out a cracker.

Annelise: Would you like a treat?

Polly: Polly want a cracker. Graaak! Polly want a cracker, pronto.

Annelise: Polly, what can you tell me about the robbery?

Polly: Now I have diamonds. I must get back to my room, pronto. Graaak! Graaak! Now I have the diamonds. I must get back to my room, pronto. Graak!

Annelise: I know who did this. The butler did it!

Mr. Moneypenny: I find that difficult to believe. Jules is very trustworthy.

Annelise: The first clue is that Crawford did not bark. That makes me think that a person who lives in this house did it.

Mr. Moneypenny: That's possible. But I need more evidence.

Annelise: The second clue is what Polly the Parrot said. Parrots always use words that they hear. She kept using the word *pronto*. I heard Jules say that same word.

Narrator 1: Mr. Moneypenny called the police right away. When the police arrived, the butler confessed to the crime, pronto.

Narrator 2: Jules went to jail. Annelise the Animal Detective had done it again! And Polly finally got that cracker.

The Haunted Tree House

> ## Characters
> - Narrator 1
> - Narrator 2
> - Gary
> - Lucy
> - Felipe
> - Megan

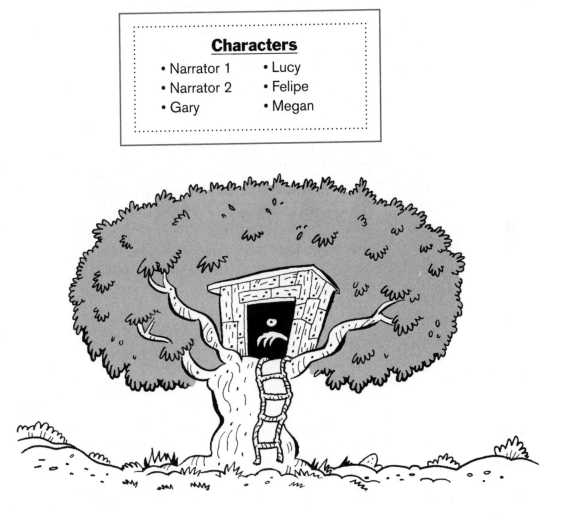

Narrator 1: The four friends had enjoyed a great summer day. It was almost evening, and the shadows were growing longer and creeping out across the lawns.

At the end of Gary's street, there was a house where an older couple lived. The couple's son was all grown up and he'd moved away many years ago. His tree house was still there, however, halfway up an oak in the backyard. Everyone said that this tree house was haunted. The four friends decided it was a perfect time for an adventure.

Gary: Let's go check out that tree house. The last one up is a rotten vulture's egg.

Narrator 2: Gary ran ahead. He started to climb the old rope ladder. Then he saw that something was inside the tree house. He could see an eye! Gary got scared. He climbed back down the ladder and ran back to his friends.

Gary: Something is hiding in the tree house. I'm not sure exactly what's up there, but it looks dangerous. I could see its big, red, angry eye looking out at me.

Lucy: That's silly. I'm not afraid. I will climb the ladder and take a look.

Narrator 1: Lucy began to climb the ladder. Her three friends stood across the yard, watching from a safe distance. When she was about halfway up, she saw a claw! What kind of terrifying creature could it belong to?

Lucy became frightened. She backed down the ladder as quickly as she could and raced back to her friends.

Lucy: There's a monster in the tree house! I could see its sharp claws.

Gary: I saw it, too. It stared right at me with its one terrifying, red eye.

Felipe: This is the goofiest thing I've ever heard in my whole life. I'll climb that ladder, peek into that tree house, and take a look for myself.

Narrator 2: Felipe started to climb the ladder. Then he saw something inside the tree house. He saw a tail all covered in fur. Felipe got very scared. He climbed back down the ladder and ran back to his friends.

Felipe: There's definitely a monster in that tree house. It has a long snakelike tail and it's all covered in thick fur.

Lucy: I saw it, too. The monster has claws like a lion.

Gary: I certainly saw it. The monster stared right at me with its one, single, horrifying, red eye, and I think it was just about to pounce.

Megan: I think you are getting each other all worked up. I'm not scared. I'm going to take a look for myself.

Narrator 1: Megan climbed the ladder all the way up to the tree house. As she was peeking inside, something came darting out.

Narrator 2: It was not a monster. It wasn't big or scary. It was little and furry.

Megan: Okay, everybody. It is safe to come up to the tree house. It was only a squirrel. The squirrel will like the three of you because you are all nuts!

Paul Bunyan

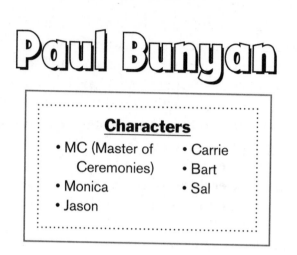

Characters

- MC (Master of Ceremonies)
- Monica
- Jason
- Carrie
- Bart
- Sal

MC: Welcome to the first annual tall-tale telling contest. We have five participants. They are named Monica, Jason, Carrie, Bart, and Sal. These five folks will be competing to see who is best at telling the story of Paul Bunyan. The winner will receive one million dollars! Why don't you get us started, Monica?

Monica: I want to tell you about how Paul Bunyan was born. It took five storks just to carry him home to his parents.

Jason: He cried so loud that animals in the woods had to hold their ears. His parents put him in a boat just to rock him to sleep.

Carrie: He was always hungry. His parents had to feed him a bathtub full of applesauce every hour. Otherwise, the rumbling from his stomach would knock down the house like an earthquake.

Bart: After one week, Paul Bunyan could fit into his father's clothes. After two weeks, he wore special clothes made out of a tent. After three weeks, he grew a beard!

Sal: By the time he was a teenager, he had grown to be 20 feet tall. At school, they made him a humongous desk and cut a hole in the roof so his head could stick out.

Monica: Paul Bunyan grew up to be a lumberjack. He could cut down ten tall trees at one time.

Jason: It was hard work. The winters were very cold. Sometimes it was so cold that people's words froze in the air. In spring, the words would unfreeze. The air would be full of talking.

Carrie: One winter, Paul Bunyan found a little baby blue ox trapped in the snow. He brought it back to the logging camp. Right away, the ox began to grow. People could actually see it growing right before their eyes. Soon, the ox was so big that it would take a crow a whole day to fly from one horn to the other.

Bart: Paul Bunyan named his new pet Babe. He made Lake Michigan just so it would have a drinking hole.

Sal: After Paul Bunyan and his men cut down trees, they used rivers to carry the logs. There was one river that was incredibly twisty. So Paul hitched Babe the Ox to one end of the river. Babe pulled it straight.

Monica: After a long day of work, Paul Bunyan would be really tired. He always wanted to sleep. But it might still be daylight. So Paul Bunyan would hold his big hand up in front of the sun. The shadow was so big it felt like nighttime. Then he could go to sleep.

Jason: One time a bee was flying near Paul Bunyan's ear. He slapped at the bee. You could feel the wind from his hand down in Texas.

Carrie: Paul Bunyan's favorite food was flapjacks. He would cook them in a giant griddle so big you could not even see across it. To get the griddle ready, five men would put pork rinds on the bottom of their shoes like ice skates. They would skate around the griddle, covering it with grease.

Bart: One time Paul Bunyan decided he wanted some popcorn. He poured 100 bags of corn onto the griddle. Soon popcorn filled the air. People thought it was snowing. But it was the middle of summer.

Sal: Some people say Paul Bunyan is still walking around with his giant ox, Babe. When you hear thunder, he is clearing his throat. If you see lightning, he is sharpening his axe on the side of a mountain.

MC: Those were great stories, everybody. It is hard to pick a winner. So I think I will declare this a five-way tie. But the prize is not a million dollars. We are actually giving away smiley-face stickers. After all, this was a tall-tale contest, right?

Rip Van Winkle

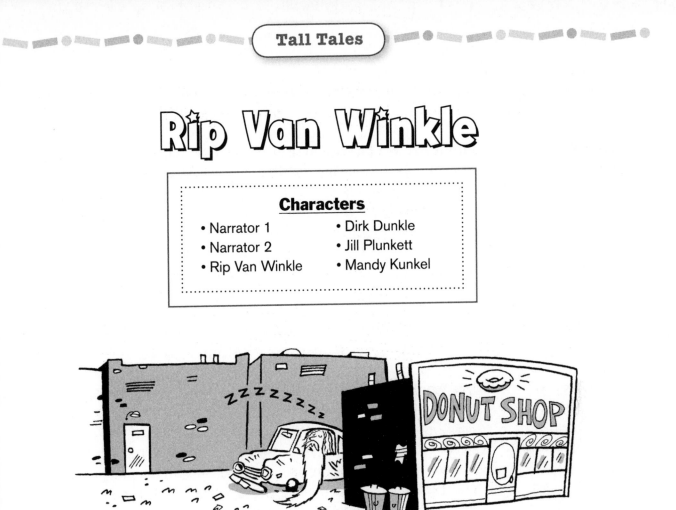

Characters
- Narrator 1
- Narrator 2
- Rip Van Winkle
- Dirk Dunkle
- Jill Plunkett
- Mandy Kunkel

Narrator 1: Rip Van Winkle is a very famous tall tale. It is also a very old-fashioned story. The story takes place more than 200 years ago. So we are going to perform a modern version of Rip Van Winkle.

Narrator 2: Rip Van Winkle worked at a donut shop. He was a very lazy man. There were only two things Rip Van Winkle enjoyed. He liked to tell stories. He also liked to sleep.

Rip Van Winkle: I sure am tired of making donuts. I think I'll slip out the back door and sneak down the alley. I know a secret place. There's a mattress inside a broken-down old car. I'll take a nice nap there, and no one will bother me.

Narrator 1: Several hours went by and Rip Van Winkle had not returned to his job at Dunkle's Donuts. The boss, Dirk Dunkle, started inquiring about him.

Dirk Dunkle: Where is Van Winkle? The donuts are not going to make themselves. He had better get back here in a hurry.

Narrator 2: Rip Van Winkle could not hear Dirk Dunkle. He was hidden away inside the old car. He just kept on sleeping.

Narrator 1: Two whole weeks passed. Rip Van Winkle did not come back to work. Everyone at Dunkle's Donuts wondered what had happened to him. Jill Plunkett was his best friend at work. She left a message on his cell phone.

Jill Plunkett: Hey Rip, where are you? Where did you go? Dirk Dunkle is really mad. But I miss goofing around at work with you. I miss hearing your silly stories. If you get this message, call me back.

Narrator 2: Rip Van Winkle did not hear his phone ring. He was still hidden inside the old car. He just kept on sleeping.

Narrator 1: Two whole years passed. The story of Rip Van Winkle was featured on a news broadcast.

Mandy Kunkel: We will now turn to the mysterious story of Rip Van Winkle. He worked at Dunkle's Donuts. One day, he simply disappeared. Mr. Van Winkle was known to be a very lazy man. Many people think that he is simply goofing off somewhere. If you have information about Mr. Van Winkle, please contact the authorities. This is Mandy Kunkel for Eyewitness News!

Narrator 2: Rip Van Winkle just kept sleeping and sleeping and sleeping.

Narrator 1: Twenty whole years passed. Suddenly, Rip Van Winkle woke up. When he touched his face, he was shocked. He now had a long beard. When he walked around, he was even more alarmed. Everything had changed. All the cars on the street looked like space ships. He walked back to Dunkle's Donuts. There was a sign that read, "Our donuts are laser-cooked for maximum flavor."

Rip Van Winkle: This certainly is odd. I think I must still be sleeping. This must be some weird dream.

Narrator 2: It was then that Rip Van Winkle saw his boss. Dirk Dunkle looked very old. All his hair had turned gray. He looked very, very angry.

Rip Van Winkle:	What time is it?
Dirk Dunkle:	It is three in the afternoon.
Rip Van Winkle:	I'm truly sorry. I must have lost track of time. I didn't mean to miss two hours of work.
Dirk Dunkle:	You did not miss two hours of work. You were gone for 20 years!
Narrator 1:	Rip Van Winkle was shocked. Apparently, he had just awoken from a 20-year nap. That explained everything. For a moment, his mouth hung open in amazement.
Narrator 2:	But then Rip Van Winkle started talking. He always had something to say. He was always talking, at least when he was awake.
Rip Van Winkle:	I'm really sorry that I missed 20 years of work. You'll never believe what happened. Boy, do I ever have a story to tell. Don't worry about the work time I missed. Maybe I can work a double-shift on Tuesday....

Mississippi Mosquitoes

Characters
- Narrator
- Angela
- Eric
- Alligator
- Mosquito #1
- Mosquito #2

Narrator: Eric was really excited. He and his family were on vacation in Mississippi. He was getting a chance to visit his cousin, Angela. He loved how different things were in Mississippi than where he normally lived. One night after dinner, Angela suggested they should take a walk along the riverbank.

Angela: It is so cool. We'll probably see all kinds of birds and turtles. If we are lucky, we'll spot some alligators.

Eric: I wouldn't mind seeing an alligator from a great distance. They're fierce, right? I wouldn't want to mess with one of those critters.

Angela: Alligators are dangerous. That's for sure. But what you do not want to mess with is a Mississippi Mosquito.

Narrator: Eric and Angela walked along for a while. All of a sudden, they heard a huge commotion in the river. They could see a big alligator thrashing and splashing in the water.

Alligator:	Oh please, I beg you! Leave me alone, you hideous bug! Desist at once, dreaded insect! Help! Help! I am in peril!
Angela:	Do you see what I see? A giant mosquito is biting that alligator.
Eric:	That's the largest mosquito I've ever seen. It's the size of a small car.
Angela:	I think we had better turn around.
Eric:	I agree. Don't mind me if I take off running at tremendous speed.
Narrator:	Suddenly, two big shadows swooped across Eric and Angela. In the next instant, they were carried up into the air.
Angela:	Help! Help! A giant mosquito has me.
Eric:	Oh, no! This is bad news! I'm being attacked by a huge mosquito!
Mosquito #1:	Correction. We are small mosquitoes. Do not worry. We will not hurt you.
Mosquito #2:	Yes, I am just a young mosquito. I am only about half-grown. So you should not be scared.
Mosquito #1:	We are going to carry you away to a safe place.
Mosquito #2:	We are trying to help you. We want to make sure that none of the big mosquitoes gets you.
Narrator:	The mosquitoes carried the two kids a long way, then put them down gently in Angela's front yard. The next day, Angela suggested they should go see a movie. A movie would be indoors, air conditioned, and have no mosquitoes. That wasn't very different from Eric's normal life. But that sounded just fine to him.

Pecos Bill

Narrator:　Some old cowboys and cowgirls were sitting around a campfire. They were telling stories. They began talking about Pecos Bill. According to their stories, he was the greatest, fastest, toughest cowboy ever. The more they talked, the taller their tales got. Their stories grew downright outrageous. But each of the old cowboys and cowgirls claimed to know Pecos Bill personally. So their stories simply had to be true.

Barb Wire: When Bill was a baby, his family was crossing the Pecos River in a wagon. He fell out, but his parents did not notice. Bill stayed behind. He was really thirsty. So he drank the Pecos River. That is how he got the name Pecos Bill.

Dry Desert Dan: He told me once that coyotes raised him. His best friend was a bear. They wrestled all the time. Pecos Bill tried not to hurt the bear.

Old Bo: After many years, Pecos Bill was found by his long-lost brother. Pecos Bill was still living with the coyotes. He would throw back his head and howl instead of speaking. His brother taught him how to talk.

Wild Jill Hiccup: I met Pecos Bill when he had just become a cowboy. He was like no cowboy I'd ever seen before. He rode a mountain lion instead of a horse. He wore a live rattlesnake as a belt.

Barb Wire: I saw Pecos Bill win a lasso contest. The first cowboy threw his lasso around a tree that was one mile away. The next cowboy lassoed a tree that was two miles away. Pecos Bill threw his lasso high into the air and caught the moon.

Dry Desert Dan: I was with Pecos Bill when he met his wife. Her name was Slue-Foot Sue. He saw her riding down a river on a giant catfish. It was the size of a whale. He lassoed Slue-Foot Sue. He pulled her right off that catfish and they got married that day.

Old Bo: That's nothing. I'll tell you about the time I heard Pecos Bill sing. His cowboy song was so calm that it put all the cattle to sleep. When we woke up the next morning, the cows were still sleeping. They would not wake up no matter how much noise we made. For the next several days, we herded sleepwalking cows.

Wild Jill Hiccup: Your boring stories are about to put me to sleep. One time I was with Pecos Bill when he heard a cattle stampede starting up. This stampede was three states away. But his ears were so sharp he could hear a flea's burp. Pecos Bill took the saddle off his mountain lion. He went and found a cyclone. Then he put his saddle on the cyclone and rode away at tremendous speed. He arrived just in time to stop the stampede.

Narrator: Suddenly, the old cowboys and cowgirls heard a shuffling sound. It was coming from over where they had tied up their horses for the night.

Phillybuster: Excuse me. I'd like to offer my two cents.

Barb Wire: A talking horse! I cannot believe my ears.

Dry Desert Dan: Somebody pinch me. I must be dreaming!

Old Bo: What in tarnation? I'm fit to be tied!

Wild Jill Hiccup: This is the rootinest, tootinest thing I ever did hear!

Phillybuster: That's right. I'm a talking horse, and I knew Pecos Bill. I don't think any of you ever even met Pecos Bill. Your silly stories are making my mane stand on end. Now, I'll tell you a real Pecos Bill story. I remember one time he was hungry for pancakes. But it was three in the afternoon. Cookie refused to make pancakes so late in the day.

So Pecos Bill simply stopped the earth. Then he used his stirrup to spin the earth backwards, faster and faster. Pretty soon, time was moving in reverse. Pecos Bill kept going until it was back to morning. Then he ordered up a plate piled 50 feet high with pancakes and ate them in one gulp. Now that's a story! I'd keep talking, but my voice is a little "hoarse."

Johnny Appleseed

> ## Characters
> - Alex Treblock
> - Christine
> - Brent
> - Vanna Brite
> - Garrett
> - A.J.

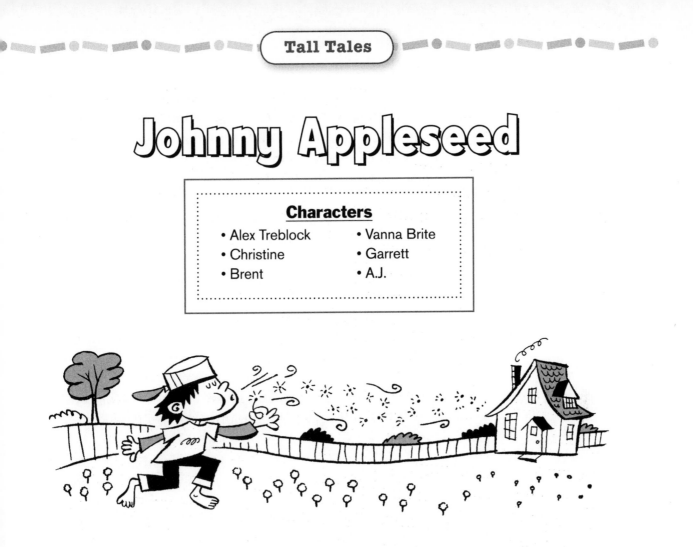

Alex Treblock: It is time to play America's most popular television game show. It is time for *Tricky Tall Tales*. I am your host, Alex Treblock. Here's my co-host, Vanna Brite. Today, we are going to tell four tall tales to four kids. Have these tall tales ever been told before? Did we make them up just for this game show? I'm going to start with Christine. Christine, what is your favorite season?

Christine: I like summer the best. It is warm outside. I get to ride my bike and go swimming.

Alex Treblock: Sounds like you really love summer, Christine. You must have heard the story of Johnny Watermelonseed. A long time ago, Johnny walked all over America, spitting watermelon seeds onto people's lawns. The seeds grew into millions of plump watermelons.

Christine [hits buzzer]: That's a made-up tall tale. I have never heard a story about Johnny Watermelonseed.

Alex Treblock: That is correct, Christine. Congratulations, you have just won a lifetime's supply of watermelons. Now, let's meet our next contestant, Brent. Brent, what is your favorite color?

Brent: I love the color yellow. Right now, I am wearing yellow socks and yellow shoes.

Alex Treblock: You certainly do love yellow, Brent. So I bet you have heard the story of Johnny Dandelionseed. He was famous for sneaking into people's yards and blowing around those little dandelion parachutes. They would float in the wind and dandelions would grow everywhere.

Brent *[hits buzzer]*: That is my favorite folktale. I have heard the story of Johnny Dandelionseed a hundred times. I could never forget it.

Alex Treblock: I'm sorry, Brent. You have been totally tricked by a tall tale. There is no Johnny Dandelionseed. Now, I'm going to turn the show over to my co-host, Vanna Brite. She has two more tall tales.

Vanna Brite: Our next contestant is Garrett. Garrett, will you tell me what state you come from?

Garrett: I am from Florida. I just want to say hello to Bucky and Lou and Grandma and Cousin Ed and my dog, Spike.

Vanna Brite: So you're visiting from Florida, Garrett. It sounds like you know everybody in the entire state. Now, Florida is known for its delicious oranges. Surely you must know the story of Johnny Orangeseed. Johnny Orangeseed drove everywhere in a bright orange mini van. He would roll down the windows and toss out seeds as he rode down the highway.

Garrett: That tall tale sounds very familiar. I think it was once told to me by my cousin's best friend's sister, Donna.

Vanna Brite:	I'm sorry, Garrett. You have just been totally tricked by a tall tale. Time to move on to our last contestant, A.J. I understand that A.J. is your nickname.
A.J.:	That's right. My name is Andrea Jane. But everybody calls me A.J.
Vanna Brite:	A.J., maybe you will recognize this tall-tale character by his famous nickname. John Chapman was born in Massachusetts in 1774. When he grew up, he wore a tin pot on his head. He walked all over America, planting apple trees. Soon everyone started calling him Johnny Appleseed.
A.J. *[hits buzzer]*:	That is a real tall tale. I am sure of it. I have heard it many times before.
Vanna Brite:	You are right. As a prize you get a special frozen apple ice cream pie sundae milkshake with whipped cream and a slice of apple on top. Your parents must be very smart, because they say the apple does not fall far from the tree! Well, that is all the time we have. Tune in next week for *Tricky Tall Tales*.

The Fearsome Four vs. the Giant Paperboy From Outer Space

> ### Characters
> - Narrator
> - Giant Paperboy
> - Captain Marble
> - Tongue Depressor
> - Spicy Mustard Man
> - Mega Pencil

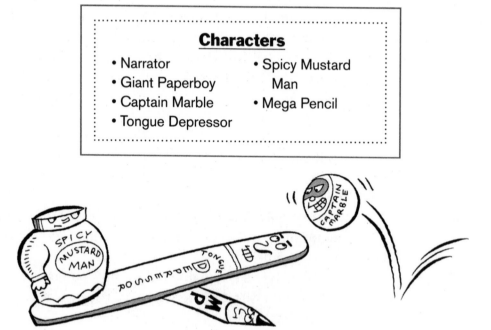

Narrator: Captain Marble, Mega Pencil, The Tongue Depressor, and Spicy Mustard Man were a team of superheroes. Together, they were known as the Fearsome Four. At least, that was the nickname they had given themselves. Nobody was sure what super feats they had actually accomplished. But one thing was for sure. The world was depending on them now. A giant paperboy had attacked from outer space. The Fearsome Four needed to come up with a plan. And they needed to come up with it fast.

Giant Paperboy: Extra, extra, read all about it! Giant Paperboy starts new route today on the planet Earth!

Captain Marble: Not so fast, Paper Fiend. I will roll under your foot and cause you to lose your balance. I've done it before and I'm not afraid to do it again.

Giant Paperboy:	News flash, Captain Marble! From my great height, you appear to be about the size of a speck of dust. You are powerless against me.
Tongue Depressor:	You are right where I want you, Paperboy. Just keep on talking. I am going to force you to open your mouth wide.
Giant Paperboy:	Stop the presses! It's a real live walking and talking tongue depressor! What's next? Is Super Doctor going to make me take some yucky medicine?
Spicy Mustard Man:	Oh, you will be taking some medicine, all right. Wait until the next time you eat a hot dog. I will sneak in there. I will mix together with the regular mustard. You will never even see me. Then, surprise! I am so spicy your future children will taste me!
Giant Paperboy:	Clarification: I don't eat hot dogs. I don't even like mustard. So what's plan B, you silly yellow blob?
Mega Pencil:	I think you should know something, Giant Paperboy. I am writing down every word you say.
Giant Paperboy:	Then how about an exclusive, Mega Pencil? See this big bag I'm carrying? It's full of giant newspapers. I am about to begin my route. I will be delivering copies of the morning edition to houses all over the world. Let's just say I may break a few windows ... or roofs.
Captain Marble:	This Giant Paperboy from outer space is a formidable foe. I do not think any one of us is strong enough to defeat him alone. We must join forces.
Tongue Depressor:	Good thinking, Captain Marble. But we must act quickly. We don't have much time.
Spicy Mustard Man:	The whole world is depending on us. We have to do something.
Mega Pencil:	Hold on, everybody. I think I've got it. I have a plan!

The four superheroes *[together]:*	We are the Fearsome Four. Alone, we're less. Together, we're more.
Narrator:	Here was the plan. Mega Pencil lay down on the ground. Tongue Depressor was positioned across the top of Mega Pencil. This formed something that looked like a seesaw. Spicy Mustard Man sat on the end of Tongue Depressor, who was resting on the ground. Captain Marble was supposed to hop onto the other end. That would shoot Spicy Mustard Man high into the air.
Mega Pencil:	Let's do it!
Captain Marble:	Here I come! Initiate Fearsome Four Airborne Spicy Mustard Save-the-World Plan.
Tongue Depressor:	Ouch!
Spicy Mustard Man:	Wheeeeeeeeeeeeee!
Narrator:	Captain Marble landed square on one end of Tongue Depressor, who was balanced on Mega Pencil. That caused the other end to fly up, just like a seesaw. Spicy Mustard Man was launched into the air. He flew and flew until all that was visible was a tiny yellow glob high in the sky. Then he landed—*splat!*—right in the Giant Paperboy's eye.
Giant Paperboy:	Terrible news! My eye is burning! How can I possibly deliver my route if I cannot see a thing?
Narrator:	The Giant Paperboy wiped Spicy Mustard Man out of his eye. With tears streaming down his cheek, he returned to outer space. The Fearsome Four had done it. They had saved the world! The powerful Paperboy had made his last dangerous delivery.

Slow Sports Network

Characters
• Bob Boomer • Commercial Announcer #1
• Pat Prattle • Commercial Announcer #2
• Lenora Loud
• Jeff Jabbersworthy

Characters
- Bob Boomer
- Pat Prattle
- Lenora Loud
- Jeff Jabbersworthy
- Commercial Announcer #1
- Commercial Announcer #2

Bob Boomer: Good evening, sports fans. This is Bob Boomer with SSN, the Slow Sports Network. Other TV networks show fast-moving sports. Here at channel 123 we cover only super-slow sports.

Pat Prattle: Tonight we have a real treat. This is an event like nothing that you have ever seen. We are proud to bring you a race between a turtle and a sloth. Which one will win? This is going to be great!

Bob Boomer: Let me set the scene for our viewers at home. The sloth is a furry mammal with long arms and legs. The turtle is a reptile with a hard shell. They are fierce rivals. They are intense competitors.

Pat Prattle: This evening, we will bring you the whole race. Do not worry, you will not miss a moment of action. The race is about to begin. Let's go to Lenora with a live report from down at the track.

Lenora Loud:	Thanks, Pat. This is Lenora Loud. I am standing down near the starting line. The sloth looks ready to run. He is wearing a jersey with a red number one. The turtle can barely hold back. She is wearing a jersey with a blue number two. But here is the bad news. There can be only one winner!
Bob Boomer:	Thank you for that report, Lenora. So what is going to happen? Will the sloth dash across the finish line first? Will the turtle pull ahead and snatch victory from the sloth? Stay tuned for all the action right after this commercial.
Commercial Announcer #1:	Some ketchup is thin and runny. Not Bo's Ketchup. Do you enjoy ketchup on a burger or hot dog? Then try Bo's. You may have to wait and wait and wait for it to pour out of the bottle. But it's worth the wait. Next time you are at the store, pick up some Bo's Ketchup. Remember, Bo's Ketchup is slow, but it is so good!
Pat Prattle:	We're back. If you are just now joining us, quite a race is about to begin. The sloth, covered in fur and wearing a red number one, has never been more ready. The turtle, covered in a shell and wearing a blue number two, is set to go.
Bob Boomer:	And they're off! This is an incredible event. You can hear the roar of the crowd. You can feel the tension. Two sleek creatures, born and bred for competition, are running the race of their lives. Let's now join Jeff Jabbersworthy.
Jeff Jabbersworthy:	Ladies and gentlemen, I have never seen anything like it. This is the sport of racing the way it's meant to be. This is pure drama! This is pure excitement! There goes the sloth. If my eyes don't deceive me, he has just taken a step. The turtle simply won't be intimidated. She has just pulled her head out of her shell! Now what? She has taken a step. She could go all the way! Now back to you, Pat.
Pat Prattle:	I have watched hundreds of races between sloths and turtles. I have to be honest. This may be the best one ever. There are so many twists. There are so many turns. We'll be right back. Don't go anywhere. You don't want to miss a second of this race.

Commercial
Announcer #2: Try new Slow Shampoo. Ordinary shampoos leave your hair looking limp and lifeless. But just think about it. You spend only about two minutes washing your hair. With new Slow Shampoo, you spend an entire day rubbing suds into your scalp. If you have the time, we have a shampoo for you. Buy new Slow Shampoo.

Bob Boomer: We're back. This is an amazing race. Let me fill you in on what happened during the commercial. The sloth took another step. Meanwhile, the turtle has stopped to chomp on some rotten lettuce. But she looks like she may take another step at any moment.

Pat Prattle: Boy, this is a great race. I'm just glad I get a chance to see it with my own eyes. Otherwise, I might not have believed it. In just six or seven more short weeks, we should know who the winner is. After that, we'll go to our next sport. We will be watching paint dry. So stay tuned.

Some Wisdom Is Dumb

Characters

- Narrator 1
- Narrator 2
- Haley
- Guru Steve
- Zarloona, Sage of the Mountain
- Ancient One

Narrator 1: It was a big day. Haley was planning to climb a mountain near her home. The mountain was not huge. She would not need any kind of special tools to climb. But it was going to be a challenge.

Narrator 2: At the base of the mountain, Haley noticed there was a table set up. There was a sign that read: "Free mountain-climbing tips from Guru Steve." A man in a suit and necktie was sitting at the table.

Haley: I might as well give this a try. What can it hurt? Maybe Guru Steve will have some good advice.

Guru Steve: Thanks for stopping by my table. I will now reveal to you the key to climbing this mountain. Most people think it is a physical task, but climbing this mountain is strictly mental. It's all in your head. I want you to visualize the mountain in your mind.

What kind of trees and flowers will you see as you walk up the path? What will the view at the top look like?

Haley: This seems like an interesting exercise, Guru Steve. Thanks for the tips. Now I think I will go and climb this mountain.

Guru Steve: Are you kidding? You are in no way mentally prepared. Before you even set foot on this mountain, you need to spend hours visualizing it in your mind's eye.

Narrator 1: Haley thanked Guru Steve again. Then she moved along. She wanted to get started climbing. But Haley had only walked a few steps when she saw a little booth.

Narrator 2: The booth had a sign that read: "Zarloona, Sage of the Mountain." Guru Steve hadn't exactly been helpful, but maybe Zarloona could offer some wisdom.

Zarloona: Welcome, young lady. What is your human name?

Haley: Er … I'm Haley. I am planning to climb this mountain. Do you have any advice for me?

Zarloona: Well, Haley, I hope you don't mind, but I am going to call you by your animal name. I will call you Terablina. Now Terablina, you should know that you cannot climb this mountain in your human form. You must get in touch with your inner animal. What is your favorite animal?

Haley: Let me think about that. I like dogs.

Zarloona: I knew it. I sensed that about you the moment I met you, Terablina. Now, you must transform yourself into a dog. Roll, Terablina! Roll like a dog!

Haley: But can't I just walk or run up the mountain?

Zarloona: You must take this seriously, Terablina. Dogs love to roll. Don't you think perhaps they know something that we humans do not? Don't waste precious time with preposterous questions. Roll, Terablina! Roll all the way up the mountain!

Narrator 1:	Zarloona was nearly yelling at her. Haley felt as if she almost did not have a choice. So she lay down on the ground and began rolling.
Narrator 2:	Rolling up a mountain was problematic. In fact, it was nearly impossible. Pretty soon, Haley was rolling downhill. She came to rest right in front of a little cottage. The sign outside read: "The Ancient One." Haley stood up, dusted herself off, and strode inside.
Haley:	I am trying to climb this mountain. I'm not having much luck. Maybe you have a suggestion.
Ancient One:	Please, call me the Ancient One.
Haley:	Okay, Ancient One. Do you have any advice for me?
Ancient One:	Trees grow tall. They start as little seeds. Birds fly high. First they are low. Clouds rise. Rains fall.
Haley:	That's great. But what does it mean?
Ancient One:	How can you hope to climb a tall mountain? First, you must dig a deep hole. The hole must be as deep as the mountain is high. Then you will understand. Dig deep. Then climb high. That is the path to wisdom.
Narrator 1:	Haley picked up a shovel that was hanging on the wall. She went outside and began to dig. After about an hour, Haley had made a small hole.
Narrator 2:	This was getting ridiculous. First, Guru Steve had asked her to spend hours visualizing the mountain in her mind. Next, Zarloona had changed Haley's name to Terablina and made her roll like a dog. Instead of climbing up the mountain, she had rolled down it. Now, she was getting even farther away from her goal. She was actually digging a hole, thanks to the Ancient One. Haley set down her shovel.
Haley:	Part of "wisdom" is "dumb." I think I will lace up my shoes tight. Then I will get on the path over there. And I will just climb up this mountain. So says Haley the Wise!

Welcome to Oddville

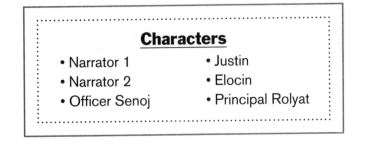

Characters

- Narrator 1
- Narrator 2
- Officer Senoj
- Justin
- Elocin
- Principal Rolyat

Narrator 1: Justin and his family moved to a new town called Oddville. The day he arrived, Justin went out for a ride on his bike. Right away, Justin knew that there was something different about this place.

Narrator 2: He noticed that nobody in Oddville was riding a bike or driving a car. He saw kids on small caribou. A family of four passed by, riding a giraffe. Suddenly, he heard a long, low growl. A police officer on a tiger signaled for Justin to pull over to the side of the road.

Officer Senoj: What are you riding? What are those two round things? I've never seen anything like it. You cannot travel the streets of Oddville on such a strange contraption. It looks extremely dangerous.

Justin: Hold on, officer. You are riding around on a tiger. Isn't that a bit dangerous?

Officer Senoj: Don't get smart with me, young man. You are clearly new in town. This time I'm going to let you off with a warning. But next time I see you, you had better be riding an ostrich or a caribou like other boys your age.

Narrator 1: On his first day in town, Justin's neighbor invited him over for dinner. Her name was Elocin. This was a very strange name. Justin thought about it for a while and realized that Elocin was Nicole spelled backwards.

Narrator 2: For dinner, Elocin's family had spaghetti and meatballs. First they plopped a few meatballs on their plates. They piled the noodles on top. Then the dove in, eating with their hands and loudly slurping noodles into their mouths. Justin used his fork.

Elocin: Where are your manners, Justin? Why are you not eating with your hands?

Justin: I do not get it. Why did you put out forks if we are not supposed to use them?

Elocin: The forks are for dessert, silly. They are for eating pudding.

Justin: You sure have some strange ways in Oddville. I was thinking about it and I figured out that people's names are backwards. In the town where I used to live, I knew two girls named Nicole.

Elocin: Nicole. That's a funny-sounding name. That's my name backwards.

Narrator 1: The next day was Justin's first day of school. He did not want to be different from everybody else. He did not want to stand out. Everything was mixed up here. Justin decided he would go right along.

Narrator 2: He dressed in an inside-out shirt, mismatched socks, backwards belt, and a big, brightly colored clown wig. He changed his name to Nitsuj and headed off to school. But the moment he arrived, Principal Rolyat rushed toward him, a worried look on his face.

Principal Rolyat: You can't wear an outfit like that to school, young man.

Justin: Why not? I am living in a town where people turn their names around backwards and eat with their hands. What is wrong with what I'm wearing?

Principal Rolyat: Those are very nice casual clothes for playing or perhaps riding an ostrich. But we have uniforms. All children are required to come to school in full scuba gear.

Narrator 1: Justin looked around. Sure enough, all the other kids were dressed this way. That is when Justin was struck by a thought. Oddville might be odd. But it was not "anything goes." The town had its own set of rules.

Narrator 2: That evening, Justin's parents took him to the store to buy a school uniform. He bought full scuba gear, including goggles and flippers. Then they all had a family dinner—roast beef and big, heaping handfuls of mashed potatoes and gravy.

News Travels Fast

Characters
- Narrator
- Newscaster
- James
- Michelle
- Aaron
- Anna

Narrator: James was getting ready for school in the morning. He turned on the TV. A newscaster was discussing the day's weather.

Newscaster: Expect a difficult morning commute. Things could get pretty messy. A large blizzard is headed toward our area. It's going to cause quite a bit of trouble.

Narrator: James misunderstood the newscaster. He thought a large lizard had escaped from a zoo. He called his friend, Michelle.

James: I was just watching the news. They are saying a big lizard is on the loose. It's headed our way. I think it must be a giant gecko or something.

Narrator: Michelle couldn't hear James very well. There were six other children in her family. They were all preparing for school and making a racket. But Michelle knew something newsworthy was about to happen. So she called Aaron.

Michelle: There's going to be an avalanche! Someone made a loud sound. It made an echo. The echo caused a stone to come loose. There's a big avalanche coming our way.

Narrator: Aaron was playing a video game while he was talking on the phone. He wasn't paying close attention. But he thought he picked up the gist of what Michelle said. He called his friend, Anna.

Aaron: There's going to be a big raffle lunch. They are going to give away all kinds of cool prizes. First prize is a trip to Ecuador.

Narrator: Anna was astounded. She dropped everything and called the television station.

Anna: This is just a rumor. It seems pretty unbelievable. But I thought I should pass along this story so your reporters can check it out. This might be important news.

Narrator: That day there was no big blizzard. There was no giant lizard. There wasn't an avalanche and neither was there a raffle lunch. But when James got home, he turned on the television again. There was a breaking news story.

Newscaster: This just in. The people of Ecuador are baffled. An evil wizard appears to be on the loose. The wizard has caused a nationwide shortage of luncheon meat. The country of Ecuador is offering a prize of precious stones to anyone who can solve this problem.

Reading Level Key*

Section 1: School Situations

The New Kid (pages 7–9)
Level 1: Narrator 2, Hannah, Danielle
Level 2: Narrator 1, Fran, Chris

The Cool Table (pages 10–12)
Level 1: Narrator 1, Narrator 2, Dylan
Level 2: Sara, Sue, Britney, Jenna

A Rumor Going Around (pages 13–15)
Level 1: Narrator 2, Davey, Janie
Level 2: Narrator 1, Daniel, Wanda

Extreme Eddy (pages 16–17)
Level 1: Narrator 2, Mrs. Cross, Mr. Fetters
Level 2: Narrator 1, Eddy, Mrs. Gillis

Borrowing Bob (pages 18–20)
Level 1: Jose, Jess, Phil
Level 2: Narrator, Bob, Isabella

Section 2: Mysteries

Who Took the Cake? (pages 21–23)
Level 1: Narrator 2, Matthew, Gwen
Level 2: Narrator 1, Dru Doppler, Sam

The Giant of Gumville (pages 24–26)
Level 1: Amber Watson, Marisa, Stu, George
Level 2: Narrator, Shirley Holmes, Marc, Emily

The DeCrunchy Code (pages 27–29)
Level 1: Zach, Voice #1, Voice #2
Level 2: Narrator, Rachel, Voice #3

Annelise, the Animal Detective (pages 30–32)
Level 1: Narrator 2, Annelise, Polly
Level 2: Narrator 1, Jules, Mr. Moneypenny

The Haunted Tree House (pages 33–35)
Level 1: Narrator 2, Lucy, Megan
Level 2: Narrator 1, Gary, Felipe

Section 3: Tall Tales

Paul Bunyan (pages 36–38)
Level 1: Monica, Jason, Bart
Level 2: MC, Carrie, Sal

Rip Van Winkle (pages 39–41)
Level 1: Narrator 2, Dirk Dunkle, Jill Plunkett
Level 2: Narrator 1, Rip Van Winkle, Mandy Kunkel

Mississippi Mosquitoes (pages 42–43)
Level 1: Angela, Mosquito #1, Mosquito #2
Level 2: Narrator, Eric, Alligator

Pecos Bill (pages 44–46)
Level 1: Barb Wire, Dry Desert Dan, Old Bo
Level 2: Narrator, Wild Jill Hiccup, Phillybuster

Johnny Appleseed (pages 47–49)
Level 1: Christine, Brent, A.J.
Level 2: Alex Treblock, Vanna Brite, Garrett

Section 4: Just For Laughs

The Fearsome Four vs. the Giant Paperboy From Outer Space (pages 50–52)
Level 1: Tongue Depressor, Spicy Mustard Man, Mega Pencil
Level 2: Narrator, Giant Paperboy, Captain Marble

Slow Sports Network (pages 53–55)
Level 1: Pat Prattle, Lenora Loud, Commercial Announcer #1
Level 2: Bob Boomer, Jeff Jabbersworthy, Commercial Announcer #2

Some Wisdom Is Dumb (pages 56–58)
Level 1: Narrator 1, Haley, Ancient One
Level 2: Narrator 2, Guru Steve, Zarloona

Welcome to Oddville (pages 59–61)
Level 1: Narrator 1, Justin, Elocin
Level 2: Narrator 2, Officer Senoj, Principal Rolyat

News Travels Fast (pages 62–63)
Level 1: James, Michelle, Aaron
Level 2: Narrator, Newscaster, Anna

* Level 1=1.0 to 2.9
  Level 2=3.0 to 4.9